HERBERT W. ARMSTRONG
& THE WORLDWIDE CHURCH OF GOD

WALTER MARTIN

BETHANY HOUSE PUBLISHERS
MINNEAPOLIS, MINNESOTA 55438
A Division of Bethany Fellowship, Inc.

Taken from *The Kingdom of the Cults* revision of 1985.

ISBN 0-87123-213-8

Published by Bethany House Publishers
A Division of Bethany Fellowship, Inc.
6820 Auto Club Road, Minneapolis, Minnesota 55438

Printed in the United States of America

DR. WALTER MARTIN holds four earned degrees, having received his education at Stonybrook School, Adelphi University, Biblical Seminary, New York University and California Western University. Author of a dozen books, a half-dozen booklets, and many articles, he has become known as "The Bible Answer Man" on a syndicated radio program heard across the United States.

Dr. Martin is founder and director of The Christian Research Institute, located in southern California and specializing in fields of biblical research and knowledge. Through the cooperation of scores of Christian scholars, ministers, missionaries and laymen, information is forwarded to the Institute for classification and use in research projects. The research consultants keep abreast of contemporary trends, both secular and theological, and provide up-to-date information in fields bearing on Christianity.

Dr. Martin, a true apologist for the Christian faith, is in great demand as a conference and seminar speaker and teacher, having lectured widely in hundreds of colleges, seminaries, universities and churches throughout the United States, Europe and Asia.

HERBERT W. ARMSTRONG AND THE WORLDWIDE CHURCH OF GOD—ANGLO-ISRAELISM

The Worldwide Church of God, founded and lead by octogenarian Herbert W. Armstrong, could more properly be designated "The New Galatianism" because of its emphasis on legalism. Since this group has media visibility throughout the entire world, it is essential that its theological system be analyzed in the light of the Word of God, to see whether or not it is, as advertised, "The Plain Truth."

To facilitate a clearer understanding of this twentieth century cult system, some historical background is necessary.

The Rise of Herbert W. Armstrong

Herbert Armstrong began his cult in this century and is its founder and present dynamic leader. The details of his early life and of the beginnings of his system are sketchy at best. Two publications by the Worldwide Church's Ambassador Press, *The Inside Story of the World Tomorrow Broadcast,* and *The Autobiography of Herbert W. Armstrong*, list some significant historical highlights of the life of Armstrong and the growth of his cult, but even these two volumes present incomplete histories. Armstrong's life before his "calling" is summarized in both publications approximately as follows. Armstrong began his professional career as an advertising and promotional man who wrote copy for the *Merchants Trade Journal* in Des Moines, Iowa (1912-1915). His whole advertising business was destroyed, however, in 1920 in what the books term "a flash depression."[1] In 1924 Armstrong

---

[1]Herbert W. Armstrong, *The Autobiography of Herbert W. Armstrong*, Pasadena, CA: Ambassador Press, 1967, vol. 1, p. 234.

moved to the Pacific Northwest where twice his business ventures failed, due to "forces beyond Mr. Armstrong's control."[2]

Mr. Armstrong's spiritual odyssey was launched primarily through his wife's discovery that "obedience to God's spiritual laws summed up in the Ten Commandments is necessary for salvation. Not that our works of keeping the commandments save us, but rather that sin is the transgression of God's spiritual law. Christ does not save us in our sins but from our sins. We must repent of sin, repent of transgressing God's law which means turning from disobedience as a prior condition to receiving God's free gift."[3]

Mr. Armstrong's Sunday school days had taught him that there are no works to salvation . . . God's law was done away with. To him religion had not been a way of life but a mere belief, an acceptance of the fact of God's existence, Christ's virgin birth, the efficacy of Christ's shed blood. Controversy arose between Mr. and Mrs. Armstrong. She refused to give up the truths she had found. He was angered into his first real study of the Bible, undertaken for the avowed purpose of proving to his wife that "all these churches can't be wrong."[4]

Armstrong's long solitary study of the Scriptures led him to the same conclusions he had fought so bitterly against with his wife. Ambassador Press publications indicate that Armstrong's struggle to change from "traditional" Christian belief to this new-found "legalism" caused within him "a furious inner struggle."[5]

After the study of his Bible and much prayer, we are informed, Mr. Armstrong began writing and doing evangelical work. It was in June of 1931 that Armstrong conducted an evangelistic campaign in Eugene, Oregon, and at that time was "ordained as a minister of Jesus Christ."

His tremendous zeal, tireless energy, writing, speaking and promotional ability stood Armstrong in good stead through the years and culminated in the founding of the Ambassador College, located in Pasadena, California; *Plain Truth Magazine,* which was started in February 1934; and *The World Tomorrow Program,* which originated in Eugene, Oregon, January 1934.

Of all the cultic structures, the Worldwide Church of God sponsors more radio broadcasts and television programs on more sta-

[2]*Ibid.,* p. 284.
[3]*Ibid.,* pp. 281-284, 286ff.
[4]Roderick Meredith, *The Inside Story of the World Tomorrow Broadcast,* Pasadena, CA: Ambassador Press, n.d., p. 47.
[5]*Ibid.,* p. 48.

tions than any other cultic group in the world, and in fact more than its five top competitors combined! Herbert Armstrong has made it a career to become a senior statesman of diplomacy for his church, and visits the various leaders of established and emerging nations, attracting their attention by his expensive gifts and direct aid programs in areas where the individual country may be in need.

An example of Armstrong's diplomacy is his high standing with the Israeli government, for whom he has sponsored archeological digs, not the least of which are his much-publicized excavations around and underneath the site of the second temple in Jerusalem.

The Armstrong religion is strong in England, throughout the United Kingdom, and on the European continent, as well as in the United States. It should be noted that Radio Luxembourg and other stations beam Armstrong's material all over Europe and behind the Iron Curtain, so the work of the Worldwide Church of God is not strange to them.

The Eclecticism of Herbert W. Armstrong

Armstrong's biographer, Roderick Meredith, goes to great pains to point out that "there was never any association in any way with Jehovah's Witnesses, Seventh-day Adventists, Mormons, or any such sects as some accusers have falsely claimed."[6]

1. *Seventh-day Adventism and Herbert Armstrong.*

Unfortunately for Mr. Meredith, the Seventh-day Adventist denomination has done a complete historical résumé of Herbert Armstrong and his association with them. Writing for the Ministerial Association of the Seventh-day Adventists, George Burnside states concerning Mr. Armstrong:

". . . Mr. Armstrong is an off-shoot of an off-shoot of an off-shoot of the Seventh-day Adventist church." The information from Burnside is summarized as follows.

In 1886 Elders B. F. Snook and W. H. Brinkerhoff, two ministers of the small and newly organized Iowa Conference of Seventh-day Adventist, apostatized, and with a few members formed

---

[6]*Ibid.*, pp. 48ff.; cf. *Autobiography, op. cit.*, p. 302, where Armstrong denies having attended any Seventh-day Adventist church services, although he admits becoming familiar with their literature. He also denies being a member of that denomination (*Ibid.*, p. 338).

a group of their own. They directed their work from Marion, Iowa. In 1889 they centered their work in Stanbury, Missouri, calling their company "the Church of God (Adventist)."

Mr. Armstrong joined this church and after a stormy experience with them, he reported that Mr. Duggar, in a dispute over leadership, led off a sizable part of the membership and called their group "the Church of God (Seventh-day)." Mr. Armstrong joined this off-shoot movement. Sometime later, because of Mr. Armstrong's acceptance of the British-Israelism theory and other subjects, he went out on his own and formed his own church, calling it "The World Church of God," known today as the Worldwide Church of God.[7]

Having checked the Adventists' documentation on this thoroughly, and finding it to be accurate, what Mr. Meredith glosses over lightly now takes on significance. The neighbor lady who revealed the great discovery to Mrs. Armstrong about the law of God was a former member of the Seventh-day Adventist Church and also a member of the splinter group. Mr. Armstrong's theology in many areas paralleled Seventh-day Adventism. His theology insists upon observance of the Seventh-day Sabbath, abstinence from certain articles of food as unclean, a general Adventist system of prophetic interpretation (albeit with his own peculiar modifications), his extreme legalism and the observance of feasts and new moons, and his denunciation of the doctrines of hell and eternal punishment for which he has substituted the Adventist doctrine of the annihilation of the wicked. Mr. Armstrong owes a considerable debt to Seventh-day Adventism, as he does to Jehovah's Witnesses (with whom he agrees in his denial of the doctrine of the Trinity and the bodily resurrection of Christ) and the Mormon Church (whose teaching that man may become as God was appropriated by Armstrong without even the slightest acknowledgment to Joseph Smith and Brigham Young).

Mr. Meredith seems overly eager to pass by these facts, but facts they are. His blanket dismissal "there was never any association in any way with Jehovah's Witnesses, Seventh-day Adventism and Mormons" is a clear misrepresentation of historical fact.

2. *Anglo-Israelism.*

---

[7] The above material is summarized from George Burnside's series on Herbert W. Armstrong as published in the *Bulletin of the Ministerial Association of Seventh-day Adventist Ministers.*

8

Anglo-Israelism (sometimes called British-Israelism) is, properly speaking, neither a sect nor a cult since it transcends denominational and sectarian lines and because it does not set up an ecclesiastical organization. It has existed for more than a century in the United States, having come to this hemisphere from England. Apparently it originated there shortly after the close of the Elizabethan era, its "first apostle" being Richard Brothers (1757-1824).

The most vocal proponents of the Anglo-Israelic system of Biblical interpretation in North America were James Lovell of Fort Worth, Texas, and Howard Rand of Destiny Publishers.

The teachings of these men and their followers are comparatively innocuous and free from serious doctrinal error. The chief harm results from the appeal to nationalism with its accompanying vanity and the two-fold way of salvation which some advocates have implied (see below).

a. Herbert Armstrong and Anglo-Israelism.

In addition to the two groups headed by James Lovell and Howard Rand, there were several other groups which also teach some of the doctrines of Anglo-Israelism. The largest of all these groups is headed by Herbert Armstrong, founder of the Worldwide Church of God and the World Tomorrow radio and television broadcasts.

Armstrong is also the founder of Ambassador College in Pasadena, and is by far the most well-known and widely heard and read of all Anglo-Israelite cultists. Mr. Armstrong is editor of *The Plain Truth*, a monthly magazine with a circulation of around 1,000,000 and is a strong influence in the publishing world of the cults.

The Worldwide Church of God is outside the historic Christian Church because it denies foundational Christian truth. All other forms of Anglo-Israelism (or at least the vast majority of them) maintain a guarded orthodoxy at least in the areas of the Nature of God, personal redemption, and the Person and Work of Jesus Christ.[8] However, it is very clear that the Worldwide Church of

---

[8] A few of them have taught, by implication at least, a form of salvation by physical birth into the nation Israel (i.e., Great Britain or the United States, for example) along with the usual Christian teachings of individual personal salvation. Some also have suggested some rather naive ideas, such as the belief that the city of Jerusalem in the Bible is really what we know today as Edinburg, Scotland. (See, for example, Comyns Beaumont, *Britain—The Key to World History*, London: Rider & Co., 1948.)

God and Mr. Armstrong do not share essential Bible doctrine with these other Anglo-Israelism groups. The essential doctrines of the Worldwide Church of God are absolutely heretical and without any Biblical foundation, as we shall see in the body of this chapter.

To sum up the theories of the Anglo-Israel cult in a concise manner is not difficult, and to refute them from the Scriptures as noted scholars and Biblical expositors have done many times, is essentially an elementary task. But with the advent of Herbert Armstrong's version of the old error and his utilizaton of it as a cloak for his own confusion on Biblical theology, the problem is no longer elementary, in fact, it is quite complex and deserves the careful consideration of responsible Christian ministers and laymen. For it is certain that they will be affected, sooner or later, by the plausible propaganda which flows from the Armstrong presses and out over the airwaves.

We shall deal with Anglo-Israelism, then, only as a prelude to dealing with the theology of Herbert Armstrong, with which it has now become identified in the minds of most people—in England, Canada and the United States.

The basic premise of the Anglo-Israelite theory is that ten tribes were lost (Israelites) when the Jews were captured by the Assyrians under King Sargon and that these so-called "lost" tribes[9] are, in reality, the Saxae, or Scythians, who surged westward through Northern Europe and eventually became the ancestors of the Saxons, who later invaded England. The theory maintains that the Anglo-Saxons are the "lost" ten tribes of Israel and are substituted, in Anglo-Israel interpretation and exegesis, for the Israel of the Bible.[10]

In the heyday of the British Empire, when their colonies spanned the globe under Victoria, Anglo-Israelites were in their glory, maintaining that, since the British were the lost tribes and, therefore, inheritors of the covenants and blessings of God, it was obvious that God was honoring His promises and exalting His children in the latter days.

In light of recent history, however, and the loss by Britain of virtually all her colonial possessions, Anglo-Israelites are content to transfer the blessings of the Covenant to the United States, maintaining as they do that Ephraim is Great Britain and Man-

---

[9]J. H. Allen, *Judah's Sceptre and Joseph's Birthright*. 6th ed., Boston: A. A. Beauchamp, Pub., 1918, pp. 124-145.

[10]Rev. Commander L.G.A. Roberts, *Commentary on the Book of the Prophet Isaiah*. London: The Covenant Publishing Co., Ltd., 1931, p. 159.

asseh, the United States. The fact that Ephraim is called "the exalted one" in Scripture and that Manasseh is designated as the inferior of the two, creates both historical and exegetical problems for the Anglo-Israelites. This is particularly true because the United States, the inferior (Manasseh), has now far surpassed the allegedly superior Ephraim, a minor problem that will not long forestall the cogitations and prophetic conjectures of the Anglo-Israelite's school of Biblical interpretation.

Relative to the relationship of Israel to Judah in Scripture, Anglo-Israelism maintains that Judah represents the Jews who are still under the divine curse and are not to be identified with Israel at all. In this line of reasoning, all the promises recorded in the Scripture are applied, not to a nation (Israel), which, as we have seen, is, in their system of thought, to be identified with Great Britain and the United States!

Herbert Armstrong, in dealing with this subject, enunciates the basic idea of Anglo-Israelism that Israel is to be distinguished from the Jews[11] (Judah) in these words:

> We want to impress here that Israel and Judah are not two names for the same nation.[12] They were and still are, and shall be until the Second Coming of Christ, two separated nations. The House of Judah always means Jew.
>
> This distinction is vital if we are to understand prophecy. Because most so-called Bible students are ignorant of this basic distinction; they are unable rightly to understand prophecy!
>
> The next place where the term "Jew" is mentioned in the Bible, the House of Israel had been driven out in captivity, lost from view, and the term only applies to those of the House of Judah. There are no exceptions in the Bible.[13]

It is further maintained by Anglo-Israelites that in their migration of the Mediterranean area across Europe to the British Isles, the "lost" tribes left behind them landmarks, bearing names

---

[11]"There is not a particle of evidence to support that the Jews of today are other than the house of Judah, or that they represent the lost Twelve Tribes. The evidence is clear that Israel did not rejoin the Jews" (J. Llewellyn Thomas, *God and My Birthright*, London: The Covenant Publishing Company, Ltd., n.d., p. 21). It should be noted that the Covenant Publishing Company is in no way associated with Herbert Armstrong or his teaching, does not subscribe to his beliefs, does not believe he has the correct interpretation of prophecy, and does not think he has rightly drawn conclusions concerning modern Israel in the latter days.

[12]Thomas (*Ibid.*, p. 5) states: "All Jews and Levites were Israelites, but all Israelites were not Jews or Levites."

[13]Herbert W. Armstrong, *Where Are the Ten Lost Tribes?*, Pasadena, CA: Ambassador Press, n.d., p. 8.

of the tribes. Thus, the Danube River and Danzig are clear indications to them of the Tribe of Dan.[14] The term Saxon is obviously derived from the Hebrew and means Isaac-son, or "the son of Isaac!"[15]

Another Anglo-Israel exercise in semantics is their insistence that the Hebrew term for covenant (*berith*), and for man (*ish*), is to be interpreted as meaning "the man of the covenant,"[16] a fact that would be amusing, if it were not for the unpleasant truth that the Hebrew and Anglo-Saxon tongues have as much in common as do Chinese and Pig-Latin!

Herbert Armstrong, however, who can read neither Hebrew, Aramaic nor Greek, states with dogmatic authority:

> The House of Israel is the covenant people. The Hebrew word for covenant is *beriyth*, or *berith*. . . . The Hebrew word for man is *iysh*, or *ish*. In the original Hebrew language, vowels were never given in the spellings, so omitting the vowel *e* form *berith*, but retaining the *i* in its Anglicized form to preserve the *y* sound, and you have the Anglicized Hebrew word for covenant, *brith*. The Hebrews, however, never pronounced their h's. The Jew, even today, in pronouncing the name Shem will call it Sem. Incidentally, this ancient Hebrew trait is also a modern British trait, so the Hebrew word for covenant would be pronounced, in its Anglicized form as Brit.
>
> And the word for covenant man or covenant people would therefore be British. So the true covenant people today are called the British. And they reside in the British Isles. . . .
>
> To Abraham God said, "In Isaac shall thy seed be called," and this name is repeated in Romans 9:7, and Hebrews 11:18. In Amos 7:16 they are called the "house of Isaac."
>
> They are descended from Isaac, and therefore are Isaac's sons. Drop the "i" from Isaac (vowels are not used in Hebrew spelling) and we have the modern name, Saac's sons, or, as we have spelled it in shorter manner, Saxons.[17]

It is sufficient to point out at this stage that the Hebrew words *berith* and *ish* literally mean "covenant and man," not, "men of the covenant," as Armstrong and Anglo-Israelites maintain. When

---

[14]Adam Rutherford, *Israel-Britain or Anglo-Saxon Israel*. London: publ. by author, 1936, 3rd ed. p. 36.

[15]Anon., *The Roadbuilder: God's Commonwealths, British and American*, Toronto, Canada: Commonwealth Publishers, Ltd., 1930, pp. 161ff. (See also Rutherford, p. 9.)

[16]Cf. Rutherford, *op. cit.*, p. 30.

[17]Anon., *The United States and British Commonwealth in Prophecy*, London: The Covenant Publishing Co., Ltd., n.d., pp. 17, 18.

to this is added the unbiased and impeccably researched conclusions of the venerable *Oxford English Dictionary* and every other major English work on etymology, there is absolutely no evidence or support for the Anglo-Israelite contention that there is a connection between the Anglo-Saxon tongue and the Hebrew language, the paucity of their claims becomes all too apparent.

Moreover, it should be noted that the Anglo-Israelite theory and the Worldwide Church of God both maintain that the throne of England is the throne of David. In the June 1953 issue of *The Plain Truth* appears the statement:

> Herman L. Hoeh now reveals the astonishing fact that Elizabeth II actually sits on the throne of King David of ISRAEL—that she is a direct descendant, continuing David's dynasty[18]—the VERY THRONE on the which Christ shall sit after his return . . . Elizabeth II was crowned "Queen of thy people Israel."[19] Turning to the article by Hoeh, it clearly states that: the throne upon which she was crowned (i.e., the "Stone of Scone," lodged in Westminster Abbey) is really the stone which Jacob used for a pillow, which he took with him when he departed from Bethel, and which later came under the care of Jeremiah the Prophet, who took it with him to England, where it became the Coronation Stone for the British (Davidic) dynasty.[20]

The disturbing scientific fact that the Stone of Scone has been examined and analyzed, and found to be . . . "calcareous, a sandstone of a reddish or purplish color, with heterogeneous pebbles and of Scottish origin"[21] does not deaden the enthusiasm of Anglo-Israelites, who must make Jacob a native of Scotland, and Bethel, a suburb of London, if they are to maintain the fiction that the

---

[18]Dr. Henry Hedyt of the American Board of Mission to the Jews has a letter from the Office of the Lord Chamberlain which states that no known reason exists why any assertion should be made that Her Majesty Queen Elizabeth was crowned Queen of Israel. It goes on to say that she is demonstrably not the Queen of Israel and cites a portion of the Coronation Service in which the Queen took the oath. He also has a letter from Brigadier Wieler, the Resident Governor of the Tower of London, which states clearly that in the Tower of London and in the Public Records Office no ancestral chart is known which substantiates the claim, "Yes, on the throne of England reigns a daughter of David, . . . a dynasty that has ruled Ireland, Scotland and England for over 2500 years!" Hoeh, "The Coronation Stone," *Plain Truth*, June 1953, p. 640.

[19]Richard D. Armstrong (son of Herbert W. Armstrong), "Why Was Elizabeth II crowned Queen of Israel?" in *The Plain Truth*, June 1953, p. 8.

[20]Herman L. Hoeh, "The Coronation Stone" in *The Plain Truth*, June 1953, p. 64.

[21]W. H. Smith, *The Ten Tribes of Israel Never Lost*, n.p., p. 91. Enthusiasts like Beaumont (pp. 128ff.), have no difficulty since they identify Bethel with Glastonburg and Jerusalem with Edinburgh, Scotland (*Ibid.*, pp. 259ff.).

Stone of Scone is of Middle Eastern origin.[22]

The Anglo-Israelites school of interpretation claims more than 3,000,000 adherents in England, Canada, the British Commonwealth and throughout the world, including the United States. They are found in many already-established denominations in Christian Churches and so do not constitute a separate denomination, preferring to work through all groups, instilling its propaganda and its fierce emphasis upon racial pride as a type of nationalistic leaven grounded in what is known to be a totally discredited method of scholarship and linguistic analysis.

Were it not for the fact that Herbert Armstrong has capitalized so successfully upon it as a means of inculcating his own peculiar interpretation of the Bible for almost a half-million readers and millions of listeners, we might well ignore Anglo-Israelism. But Armstrong has, in a very real sense, resuscitated what was a gradually dying theological body, and its death throes have now given way to militant life with which the Church of Jesus Christ must come to grips.

b. The Biblical Answer to Anglo-Israelism.

There are two principal areas in which the Anglo-Israel theory must either stand or fall. They are, first, the question whether any tribes *were* lost, and therefore later reappeared as the British and American nations; second, there is the question of whether or not it is possible, in either the Old or New Testaments, to teach that

> Israel and Judah are not two names for the same nation. They were and still are, and shall be until the Second Coming of Christ, two separate nations. The House of Judah always means Jew. . . . the term applies only to those of the House of Judah. There are no exceptions in the Bible![23]

Rather than become bogged down in an attempt to interpret Anglo-Israel chronology and methodology in the Old Testament, we have elected to let one of the greatest Hebrew scholars of the Christian Church, Dr. David Baron, an Englishman, answer the first question. It should be remembered that Dr. Baron's answer is substantiated in every detail by scholars of the Old Testament, whether or not they are Christian.

---

[22]Beaumont, *et. al.*, maintain the fiction that the British Isles contain the Biblical Holy Land cities.

[23]*Where Are the Ten Lost Tribes?*, op. cit., p. 8.

14

The Anglo-Israelite theory . . . I cannot help regarding as one of the saddest symptoms of the mental and spiritual shallowness of the present day. . . . I believe that you . . . like many other simple-minded Christians are perplexed and imposed upon by the plausibilities of the supposed identifications (of British Israelism), and are not able to detect the fallacies and perversions of Scripture and history upon which the whole theory is based.

Let us glance at the question of the so-called "lost" ten tribes in the light of Scripture history and prophecy. Anglo-Israelism first of all loses the ten tribes, claiming for them a different destiny from the Jews, whom it supposes to be descendants of the two tribes only. And then it identifies this "lost" Israel with the British race. But there is as little historical reason for the supposition that the ten tribes are lost, in the sense in which Anglo-Israelism uses the term, as there is scriptural basis for a separate destiny for "Israel" apart from "Judah."

The most superficial reader of the Old Testament knows the origin and cause of the unfortunate schism which took place in the history of the elect nation after the death of Solomon. But this evil was to last only for . . . a limited time; for the very commencement of this it was announced by God that He would in this way afflict the seed of David, but *not for ever* (1 Kings 11:39).

The final overthrow of the northern kingdom took place, as we have seen, in the year 721 B.C., but when we read that the "king of Assyria took Samaria and carried Israel away into Assyria," we are not to understand that he cleared the whole land of all the people, but that he took the strength of the nation with him.

Jerusalem was finally taken in 588 B.C., by Nebuchadnezzar-—just 133 years after the capture of Samaria by the Assyrians. Meanwhile the Babylonian Empire succeeded the Assyrian; but although dynasties had changed, and Babylon, which had sometimes, even under the Assyrian *régime*, been one of the capitals of the Empire, now took the place of Nineveh; the region over which Nebuchadnezzar now bore rule was the very same over which Shalmaneser and Sargon reigned before him, only somewhat extended.

With the captivity (Assyrian and Babylonian) the divisions and rivalry between "Judah" and "Israel" were ended, and the members of all tribes who looked forward to a national future were conscious not only of one destiny but that such a destiny was bound up with the promises to the house of David, and with Zion or Jerusalem as its center, in accordance with the prophecies of Joel, Amos, and Hosea, and of the other inspired messengers who ministered and testified more especially among them until the fall of Samaria. This conviction of a common and united future, no doubt, facilitated the merging process, which cannot be said to have begun with the captivity. It commenced almost immediately after the rebellion under Jeroboam, but which was certainly strengthened by it.

Glimpses into the feeling of the members of the two kingdoms for one another, and their hopes and aspirations for unity, we get in the writings of Jeremiah, Ezekiel, and Daniel, who prophesied during the period of exile. The most striking prophecy in relation to this subject is Ezekiel 37:15-17: "The word of the Lord came again unto me, saying, Moreover, thou son of man, take thee one stick, and write upon it, For Judah, and for the children of Israel his companions (that is, those of Israel who before the captivity fell away from the ten tribes and joined the southern kingdom): then take another stick, and write upon it, For Joseph, the stick of Ephraim, and for all the house of Israel his companions: and join them one to another into one stick; and they shall become one in thine hand."

Then follows the divine interpretation of this symbol: "Behold, I will take the stick of Joseph, which is in the hand of Ephraim, and the tribes of Israel his fellows, and will put them with him (or literally, I will add them upon, or to him), even with the stick of Judah, and make them one stick, and they shall be one in mine hand. And the sticks whereon thou writest shall be in thine hand before their eyes. And say unto them. Thus saith the Lord God; Behold, I will take the children of Israel from among the heathen, whither they be gone, and will gather them on every side, and bring them into their own land; and I will make them one nation in the land upon the mountains of Israel; and one king shall be king to them all: and they shall be no more two nations, neither shall they be divided into two kingdoms any more at all: neither shall they defile themselves any more with their idols, nor with their detestable things, nor with any of their transgressions: but I will save them out of all their dwelling-places, wherein they have sinned, and will cleanse them; so shall they be my people, and I will be their God. And David my servant shall be king over them; and they all shall have one shepherd; they shall also walk in my judgments, and observe my statutes, and do them. And they shall dwell in the land that I have given unto Jacob my servant, wherein your fathers dwelt; and they shall dwell therein, even they, and their children, and their children's children for ever: and my servant David shall be their prince for ever" (Ezekiel 37:19-25).

In 458 B.C. Ezra, "the scribe of the law of the God of heaven," in accordance with the decree of Artaxerxes organized another large caravan of those whose hearts were made willing to return to the land of their fathers. Part of this most favorable royal proclamation, was as follows: "I make a decree that all they of the people of Israel, and of his priests and Levites in my realm, which are minded of their own free will to go up to Jerusalem, go with thee"; and in response to it "this Ezra went up from Babylon . . .

and there went up (with him) of the children of Israel, and of the priests, and the Levites, and the singers and the porters, and the Nethinims, unto Jerusalem in the seventh year of Artaxerxes the king" (Ezra 7:13, 6, 7).

This party consisted of about one thousand eight hundred families, and apart from the priests, Levites, and Nethinims, was made up of "the children of Israel," irrespective of tribal distinctions, from all parts of the realm of "Babylon," or Assyria, now under the sway of the Medo-Persians.

The narratives contained in the books of Ezra and Nehemiah, under whose administration the position of the restored remnant became consolidated, covers a period of about 115 years, and brings us down to about 420 B.C.

Anyhow it is a fact that the remnant in the land grew and grew until, about a century and a half later, in the time of the Maccabees, and again about a century and a half later still, in the time of our Lord, we find "the Jews" in Palestine a comparatively large nation, numbering millions, while from the time of the downfall of the Persian Empire, we hear but very little more of the Israelite exiles in ancient Assyria or Babylon. By the conquest of Alexander, who to this day is a great favorite among the scattered nation, the regions of ancient Babylonia and Media were brought comparatively near and a highway opened between East and West. From about this time settlements of "Jews" began to multiply in Asia Minor, Cyprus, Crete, on the coasts of the Aegean, in Macedonia and other parts of Southern Europe, in Egypt and the whole northern coast of Africa, whilst some made their way further and further eastward as far as India and China. There is not the least possibility of doubt that many of the settlements of the Diaspora in the time of our Lord, north, south, and west, as well as east of Palestine, were made up of those who had never returned to the land of their fathers since the time of the Assyrian and Babylonian exiles, and who were not only descendants of Judah, as Anglo-Israelism ignorantly presupposes, but of all the *twelve tribes scattered abroad* (James 1:1).

As a matter of fact, long before the destruction of the second Temple by Titus, we read of currents and countercurrents in the dispersion of the "Jewish" people.

To summarize the state of things in connection with the Hebrew race at the time of Christ, it was briefly this:

I. For some six centuries before, ever since the partial restoration in the days of Cyrus and his successors, the descendants of Abraham were no longer known as divided into tribes but as one people, although up to the time of the destruction of the second temple tribal and family genealogies were for the most part preserved, especially among those who were settled in the land.

II. Part of the nation was in Palestine, but by far the larger number were scattered far and wide, and formed innumerable communities in many different lands, north and south, east and west. But wherever dispersed and to whatever tribe they may have belonged, they all looked to Palestine and Jerusalem as their center. They felt they were of the same stock, stood on the same ground, cherished the same memories, grew up under the same institutions, and anticipated the same future. They had one common center of worship in Jerusalem, which they upheld by their offerings; and they made pilgrimages thither annually in great numbers at high festivals.

The name of "Jew" and "Israelite" became synonymous terms from about the time of the Captivity. It is one of the absurd fallacies of Anglo-Israelism to presuppose that the term "Jew" stands for a bodily descendant of "Judah." It stands for all those from among the sons of Jacob who acknowledged themselves, or were considered, subjects of the theocratic kingdom of Judah, which they expected to be established by the promised "Son of David"—the Lion of the tribe of Judah—whose reign is to extend not only over *all the tribes of the land,*" but also "from sea to sea, and from the river unto the ends of the earth."

"That the name 'Jews,' " writes a Continental Bible scholar, "became general for all Israelites who were anxious to preserve their theocratic nationality, was the more natural, since the political independence of the ten tribes was destroyed." Yes, and without any hope of a restoration to a separate national existence! What hopes and promises they had were, as we have seen, linked with the Kingdom of Judah and the House of David.

Anglo-Israelism teaches that members of the ten tribes are never called "Jews," and that "Jews" are not "Israelites," but both assertions are false. Who were they that came back to the land after the Babylonian exile? Anglo-Israelites say they were only the exiles from the southern kingdom of Judah, and call them "Jews."

It is clear from the prophecies of Amos and Hosea, which were primarily addressed to the ten tribes, that if they were in the first instance "cast out" by force from their own land (as the word in the Hebrew means), it was with a view that they should be "tossed about" and "wander" among "all nations."

Now note, Anglo-Israelism tells you to identify the ten tribes with one nation, but if you are on the line of scripture and true history, you will seek for them "among all nations." He that scattered Israel will gather him, and by His own Divine power and omniscience separate them again into their tribes and families.

My last words on this subject must be those of warning and entreaty. Do not think, as so many do, that Anglo-Israelism, even if not true, is only a harmless speculation. I consider it nothing short of one of the latter-day delusions by which the Evil One seeks to divert the attention of men from things spiritual and eternal.

18

Summing up his judgments on the Anglo-Israel question relative to their methods of interpretation, Dr. Baron stated:

> One of its foundation fallacies is that it anticipates the millennium and interprets promises which will only be fulfilled in that blessed future period, after Israel as a nation is supernaturally converted. There is no way the Scriptures can be stretched to identify that Israel with the British nation at the present time. By such a faulty identification, such "interpreters" make all prophetic Scripture meaningless. It fosters national pride, and nationalizes God's blessings in this dispensation which is individual and elective in its character. It diverts man's attention from the one thing needful, and from the only means by which he can find acceptance with God. . . . After all, in this dispensation, it is a question only as to whether men are in Christ, or not. If they are Christians, whether Jew or Gentile, their destiny is not linked either with Palestine or with England, but with that inheritance which is incorruptible and undefiled, and which fades not away; and if they are not Christians, then instead of occupying their thoughts with vain speculations as to a supposed identity of the British race with the lost ten tribes, it is their duty to seek the One and only Savior, whom we must learn to know, not after the flesh, but after the Spirit, without whom a man, either an Israelite or not, is undone.
>
> And finally, it not only robs the Jewish nation, the true Israel, of many promises in relation to their future by applying to the British race in the present time, but it diverts attention from them as the people in whom is bound up the purpose of God in relation to the nations, and whose receiving again to the heart of God after the long centuries of unbelief, will be as life from the dead to the whole world.[24]

Dr. Baron's brilliant and thorough refutation cannot be improved upon. And excerpts from this personal letter which he addressed to a Christian, perplexed by Anglo-Israelite perversions of history and Biblical interpretation, remain a classic, and the letter has never been refuted by Anglo-Israelites.

The second barrier is that of the identification of Israel and Judah as separate nations, as seen by Mr. Armstrong's previously quoted statement. This matter can be summarily dismissed by careful consideration of the following facts.

First, after the Babylonian captivity, from which the Jews returned, Ezra records that the remnant were called by the name Jews (eight times), and by the name Israel, forty times. Nehemiah

---

[24]David Baron, *A Letter to an Inquirer*, London: privately published, n.d., pp. 36-38.

records eleven times that they were Jews, and proceeds to describe them as Israel, twenty-two times. The Book of Esther records their partial restoration, calling them Jews forty-five times, but never Israel. Are we to conclude that only Judah (the Jews), and not Israel, were restored under Zerubbabel and Joshua? History, archaeology and a study of Hebrew, refute this possibility completely.

The sixth chapter of Ezra describes the sin offering, mentioning specifically that ". . . twelve he goats, according to the number of the tribes of Israel" were offered for all Israel (v. 17), a fact attested to by Ezra 8:35.

While it is true that in the post-exilic period, we no longer have two kingdoms, but one nation, the prophet Zechariah describes them in comprehensive terms as "Judah, Israel and Jerusalem" (Zechariah 1:19), literally, "the House of Judah, and the House of Joseph" (Zechariah 10:6). Zechariah 8:13 identifes Judah and the House of Israel as one nation, and Malachi called the Jews Israel or Jacob, in contrast to Esau.

The coup de grace to Anglo-Israelism's fragmented exegesis is given by the prophet Amos of Judah, a man specifically set apart by God to prophesy to the ten-tribed kingdom of the North. Dr. Baron points out that he "abode in Bethel, which was a center of the idolatrous worship set up by Jeroboam . . . there his duty was to announce the coming judgment of God on the Israel of the ten tribes on account of their apostasy" (*Ibid.*, p. 34).

In the last chapter of his book, Amos in approximately 728 B.C. declares:

> Behold, the eyes of the Lord God are upon the sinful kingdom, and I will destroy it from off the face of the earth; saving that I will not utterly destroy the house of Jacob, saith the Lord. For, lo, I will command, and I will sift the house of Israel among all nations, like as a corn is sifted in a sieve, yet shall not the least grain fall upon the earth. All the sinners of my people shall die by the sword, which say, The evil shall not overtake nor prevent us (9:8-10).

We learn from this prophecy that as a kingdom, the ten tribes were to suffer destruction and their restoration would never be realized. How then is it possible for them to be "lost" for almost three millenniums, and then reappear as the British Kingdom when the kingdom was never to be restored?

The Prophet Jeremiah informs us that Israel and Judah are both declared to be "an outcast" (chapter 30), which, in combination with Isaiah 11, proves that they are considered to be one nation in both the eyes of the prophets and in the eyes of God.

Anglo-Israelism would do well to consider these facts, as would Mr. Armstrong in particular, who speaks perpetually with breathtaking dogmatism on subjects about which he apparently knows very little historically, theologically or linguistically. He therefore pours forth interpretations which can only be construed to have progressed out of the abundance of his ignorance.

Second and finally, the New Testament speaks on the subject of the equation of Israel and Judah as one nation, described alternately and interchangeably as "the Jews" and "Israel."

Peter at Pentecost, proclaims the message of redemption to "all the house of Israel." Paul in Acts 26:6 and 7 apparently took Zechariah's statement:

> And it shall come to pass, that as ye were a curse among the heathen, O house of Judah, and house of Israel; so will I save you, that ye shall be a blessing . . . (Zechariah 8:13).

In this context, Israel shall indeed be scattered among the nations, and so will Judah, and they shall be redeemed again together to bring forth a blessing in the Person of the Messiah, whose Gospel is to the Jew first, (not just to the house of Israel but as a separate nation), and also to the Gentiles (Romans 1:16b).

A cursory reading of the tenth chapter of Matthew indicates that Jesus Christ Himself considered "the lost sheep of the house of Israel," to include "the Jews," since the missionary journeys of the twelve were limited to the environs of Palestine.

It should be recalled also that Pauline theology, especially in the Book of Romans (chapters 9-11), deals specifically with Israel, not as a nation in the sense of geography, but in the sense of spiritual transgression. He refers to them as God's people who have not been cast away.

If Israel and Judah are separate nations, why then does the Apostle describe the Jews as "his brethren" and as "kinsmen according to the flesh," and then identify them as "Israelites, heirs to the promises of God," as those promises are provided for in the coming Messiah?

The Apostle Paul made this clear by declaring "I am a man which am a Jew . . . for I am also an Israelite . . . are they Israelites? So am I." (Acts 21:39; 22:3; Romans 11:1; 2 Corinthians 11:22; Philippians 3:5).

Jesus Christ sprang from Judah "a Jew," in Anglo-Israelite

reckoning, and the Apostle Paul declares in Romans that it was in Israel that "Christ came, who is God over all, blessed for ever" (9:5, Greek).

Let it not be forgotten that Anna the Prophetess was "of the tribe of Aser" (Israel), but she is called "a Jewess" of Jerusalem, facts which forever decimate the concept of Armstrong and the British Israelites that England is the throne of David and is Ephraim, while America is Manasseh.

The words of Jeremiah the Prophet conclude our observations, where he states:

> In those days, and in that time, saith the Lord, the children of Israel shall come, they and the children of Judah together. . . (50:40).

This is proof positive that both the house of Israel and the house of Judah would return from the captivity, and that as the New Testament amply demonstrates, it would be considered as one nation, no longer a kingdom in the historic meaning of that term.

Anglo-Israelism stands refuted by the facts of Scripture and history, and it would be unworthy of attention, if it were not being utilized as a tool by the Armstrong cult, which opens a Pandora's box of multiple and destructive heresies, some of which we shall consider.

c. Other Eclectic Sources and Traits of Herbert Armstrong.

Like so many other non-Christian cultists, Herbert Armstrong claims for himself a divine mandate and nowhere is this more clearly exemplified than in his own writing:

> Yet, is there *anything* so shocking—so hard to believe—as this flat Biblical statement that the whole world is religiously deceived?
>
> Thirty-seven years ago *I* simply couldn't believe it—until I found it *proved!* And even then, my head was swimming: I found myself all mixed up. To see with my own eyes in the Bible the *opposite* of what I had been taught from boyhood in Sunday school, well this was pretty hard to take, yet there it was in plain type before my eyes!
>
> If this were the year A.D. 30 and you took a trip to Jerusalem and there speaking to a throng around him you should see an ordinary looking young man about the age of 33 teaching the same things you hear me and Garner Ted Armstrong say over the raido today, it would have been just as astonishing to you then as it is today—and it was to those who heard Him then. . . . You would have been truly astonished! His doctrine was so different!

And He spoke dogmatically with assurance, with power and authority. . . . Yet He had foretold a prophecy. He had foretold wolves coming in sheep's clothing to deceive the world. He had said they would enter in profession to come in His name claiming to be Christian, yet deceiving the whole world. That happened!

For two 19-year time cycles the original apostles did proclaim this Gospel, the Gospel of the Kingdom of God, but in A.D. 69 they fled. In A.D. 70 came the military siege against Jerusalem. The ministers of Satan had wormed their way in, had gained such power that by persecution of political influence they were able to brand the true people of God as heretics and prevent further organized proclaiming to the same Gospel Christ brought from God. For eighteen and one-half centuries that Gospel was not preached. The world was deceived into accepting a false gospel. Today Christ has raised up His work and once again allotted two 19-year time cycles for proclaiming His same Gospel, preparatory to His Second Coming. . . . *The World Tomorrow* and *The Plain Truth* are Christ's instruments which He is powerfully using. Yes, His message is shocking today. Once again it is the voice in the wilderness of regilious confusion![25]

Mr. Armstrong's son, Garner Ted, once heir-apparent to his father's throne, carries the same theme through:

"No man ever spoke like this man," reported their officers to the Pharisees regarding Jesus. The multitudes "were astonished at His doctrine."

Today that same *living Christ*, through *The World Tomorrow* broadcast, *The Plain Truth* magazine, and *this Work*, proclaims in mighty power *around the world* His *same Gospel*—the *same* Gospel preached by Peter, Paul, and the original Apostles.[26]

As did Joseph Smith, "Pastor" Russell, and Mary Baker Eddy before him, so does Mr. Armstrong pose his efforts as the only work which is accurately representing Christianity today. But a tree is known by its fruit, and fruits are not only manifested in a life which is lived, but also in doctrines which are believed and taught. And so it is to the doctrines and teachings of The Worldwide Church of God that we shall now turn for a closer look at what Mr. Armstrong calls The Plain Truth.

The Theology of the Worldwide Church of God

I. *The Divine Origin Of The Worldwide Church Of God*
I'm going to give you the frank and straight answer. You have

[25]*The Inside Story. . .* , *op. cit.*, pp. 7-11.
[26]*Ibid.*, p. 2.

a right to know all about this great work of God, and about me. First, let me say—this may sound incredible, but it's true—*Jesus Christ foretold this very work—it is, itself the fulfillment of his prophecy* (Matthew 24:14 and Mark 13:10).

Astounding as it may seem, there is no other work on earth proclaiming to the whole world *this very same gospel* that Jesus taught and proclaimed!

And *listen again*! Read this twice! Realize this, incredible though it may seem—no other work on earth is proclaiming this true Gospel of Christ to the world as Jesus foretold in Matthew 24:14 and Mark 13:10! This is the most important activity on earth today![27]

The prophecies bring this Church into concrete focus in the 12th chapter of Revelation. There she is shown spiritually, in the glory and splendor of the Spirit of God, but visibly in the world as a persecuted, Commandment-keeping Church *driven into the wilderness*, for 1,260 years, through the middle ages!

In New Testament prophecy *two churches* are described.

One, the great and powerful and universal church, a *part* of the world, actually ruling in its politics over many nations, and united with the "Holy Roman Empire," brought to a concrete focus in Revelation 17.

. . . She is a *mother* Church! Her daughters are also *churches* who have come out of her, even in protest, calling themselves Protestant—but they are fundamentally of her family in pagan doctrines and practices! They, too, make themselves a *part of* this world, taking active part in its politics—the very act which made a "whore" out of their *Mother*!

The entire apostate family—Mother, and more than 500 daughter denominations, all divided against each other and in *confusion* of doctrines and festivals—has a family *name*! They call themselves "Christian," but God calls them something else—*"Mystery, Babylon the Great!"*

But the true Church of God is pictured in prophecy as the *"Little* Flock!" . . . It has kept God's festivals . . .

That Church always has existed, and it exists today!"[28]

II. *The Trinity of God and the Divinity of Man*

The *purpose* of life is that in us God is really re-creating his *own kind—reproducing himself* after His own kind—for we are, upon real conversion, actually *begotten* as sons (yet unborn) of [God]; then, through study of God's revelation in His Word, living by His every Word, constant prayer, daily experience with trials and testings, we grow spiritually more and more like God, until,

---

[27]Personal letter to Robert Sumner, November 27, 1958.
[28]Herbert W. Armstrong, *Easter Is Pagan*, Pasadena, CA: Ambassador Press, n.d., pp. 8, 9.

at the time of the resurrection we shall be instantaneously *changed* from mortal into *immortal*—we shall then be *born of* [God]—*We shall then be God!*[29]

. . . Yes, and as a *born* [son of god], Christ *is* God! God Almighty His Father is god. They are two separate and individual Persons (see Revelation 5:1, 6, 7).[30]

. . . I suppose most people think of God as one single individual Person. Or, as a *"trinity." This is not true.*

. . . But the theologians and "Higher Critics" have blindly accepted the heretical and false doctrine introduced by *pagan* false prophets who crept in, that the *Holy Spirit* is a *third person*—the heresy of the *"trinity."* This *limits* God to "Three Persons."[31]

Do you really grasp it? The *purpose* of your being alive is that finally you be *born* into the Kingdom of God, when you will actually *be God*, even as Jesus was and is God, and His Father, a different Person, also is God!

You are setting out on a training to become *creator*—to become *God!*[32]

III. *The Nature of Christ*

Jesus, *alone*, of all humans, has so far been *saved!* By the resurrective power of *God!* When Jesus comes, at the time of the resurrection of those *in Christ*, He then brings His reward with *Him!*[33]

Christ, one of the beings in the Godhead, had now been *changed* into flesh—still having the *personality* and *will* to do right which distinguished Him as an entity—yet now had become human, having *human nature* with all of its *desires, weaknesses* and *lusts*—and subject to *death* just like any other human.

This is a truth about which *millions are deceived.*

The Satan-inspired doctrine that Jesus was *not* human, that He did *not* inherit the human nature of Adam, that He did *not* have all the normal human nature of Adam, that He did *not* have all the normal human passions and weaknesses against which all of us have to struggle—in a word, that Jesus did *not* really come "in the flesh" as a normal human being—*This is the doctrine of the anti-Christ.* Notice Romans 8:3: "God sending His own Son in the likeness of sinful flesh."

The idea Satan is trying to put across is that it is *impossible* for man to keep the spiritual law of God, and so Jesus came as our Savior—not "in the flesh" with normal human nature—but

[29]Herbert W. Armstrong, *Why Were You Born?*, Pasadena, CA: Ambassador Press, n.d., pp. 21, 22.

[30]Herbert W. Armstrong, *Just What Do You Mean—Born Again?*, Pasadena, CA: Ambassador Press, n.d., p. 16.

[31]*Ibid.*, pp. 17, 19.

[32]*Why Were You Born?, op. cit.*, pp. 21, 22.

[33]*Ibid.*, p. 12.

through "special process" so that He could keep the law of God *in our stead* to *die* for us! But His *obedience* was our example!

. . . that Jesus taught, *"If* thou wilt enter into life, *keep the commandments"* (Matthew 19:17).

. . . We are not only to keep the letter of the law, but to follow it as it is magnified throughout the Bible in "every word of God" (2 Corinthians 3:6).

Satan the Devil, through His *false ministers* who appear as "ministers of righteousness" (2 Corinthians 11:13-15), is trying to deceive the world into believing in a *false Christ*—a Christ who *did away* with the Father's spiritual *law* and made it possible for us to inherit eternal life without having to build, with the help of God's Spirit, the kind of holy, righteous *character* which would enable us to obey God's eternal, spiritual *law* both now and forever.[34]

How plain! How abundantly clear! Not having *human nature* with its *passions and lusts*, God *cannot* be tempted with evil. And on the contrary, *every* man is tempted by his own *lust*—because every man does have *human nature*.

So it is not only *possible*—but *obligatory*—that we obey God's spiritual law, the Ten Commandments, as they are, magnified throughout the Bible. Keeping them in the spirit does *not* mean "spiritualizing" them away, but really obeying them as Jesus set us the example, through the power of God's Holy Spirit, which He gives to them that obey Him (Acts 5:32).

The *only difference* between Jesus and any other human is that He was conceived of the Holy Spirit. Therefore He obeyed God's laws *from birth*—and never had to go through the process of repenting of going the wrong way, of *unlearning* wrong ideas and habits, and of gradually learning to exercise His will to do right continually.

. . . And, praying for the strength He needed through the Holy Spirit, *He always* did *right*.

Yes, Jesus had *sinful* flesh—human nature. But by exercising the *will* to always obey God, and by receiving the extra help He needed to *master* His fleshly desires, Jesus *repudiated* the sway of sin in the human flesh and showed that the law of God *could be kept*.

. . . They were not worshiping Jesus as just another *Man*.

. . . Christ came *in the flesh* to set us a *perfect example*, then *to die* in payment for our sins and make it possible for us to be reconciled to a holy, righteous God and receive of His Spirit—His very *life and character* implanted within us.[35]

That is, He who had existed from eternity—He by whom God created the worlds and all things therein—He who was and is

---

[34]*The Plain Truth*, November 1963, pp. 1, 4, 7, 8.
[35]*Ibid.*, pp. 11, 12.

Life—He who was God—He *was made flesh* — converted *into flesh*, until He *became flesh* and then He *was* flesh!

Yes, Jesus was a fleshly *man*. He was God, come in human flesh. And, when converted into human flesh the *life* that kept Him alive resided *in the blood*, as in all who are *flesh* (Leviticus 17:11).

. . . But He was not God inside of, yet separate from the body of flesh—He, God, was *made flesh*, until He, still *God*—God, with us—God *in* (not inside of) the human flesh—God manifest *in the flesh* (1 Timothy 3:16).

If there was no other Person in the Godhead, then the Giver of all Life was dead and all hope was at an end!

If there was no *Father* in heaven while Jesus Christ lay dead— His blood in which resided His *life* shed from *His* veins, given for you and for me—then all life everywhere had come to an end.

. . . That's where His life resided—in His *blood*, not in spirit! He did not shed *a spirit* to save us from our sins—He shed His *blood, and* in so doing *gave His life*.

But, "as the Father hath life *in Himself*; so hath He given to the Son to have life in Himself" (John 5:26). God the Father raised Jesus from the dead. Cf. John 2.

Not Resurrected in Same Body

Now notice carefully, God the Father did not cause Jesus Christ to get back into the body which had died.

Some seem to believe that it was only the *body* which died— that Jesus Christ never died.

. . . What they believe is that a *body* Christ lived in died, but Christ *Himself* never died, Christ was God, and they argue, God could not die!

If they are right, they are lost and doomed to eternal punishment! If Christ did not die for their sins—if it was only a mortal *body which* died—then we have no Savior, and we are *lost*.

What happened is that the Logos—the *Word*—the Eternal— was *made flesh*. He was converted into—changed into flesh. Now He was flesh and blood, exactly as you and I.

His *life* was in His blood, and He gave His *life* by the fact His blood poured out while He was on the cross! He had taken on a *human* nature. He was God—but now God changed *into* flesh and blood—God with us—Emmanuel!

Yes, the Word was *made flesh*, and He was flesh and blood, not just an immortal Spirit *in* a body of flesh and blood.

It was *Christ Himself* who was *dead*. He was *revived*. Nowhere does the Scripture say He was alive and active, or that God had Him get back into the human *body*, that had died and was now resurrected.

Jesus Christ was *dead*. He was as much "out" as a boxer

27

knocked senseless—much *more*, for the boxer usually is not dead but only unconscious. Jesus was *dead*—but was *revived!*

And the resurrected body was no longer human—it was the Christ resurrected, *immortal*, once again *changed!* As He had been changed, converted *into* mortal human flesh and blood, subject to death, and for the *purpose* of *dying for our sins, now,* by a *resurrection from the dead, He was again changed, converted, into immortality*—and He is alive forevermore! Now a *living* Savior, not a *dead* Savior, He *was* dead—but only for three days and three nights.[36]

IV. *The Personality of the Holy Spirit*

God's Holy Spirit is His *life*. *It* imparts His *life* to you! *It* imparts more as we shall see!

One thing more, the Holy Spirit is *divine, spiritual love*—the love of God flowing into you from God Almighty—through the living Christ! (Romans 5:5).[37]

But the theologians and "Higher Critics" have blindly accepted the heretical and false doctrine introduced by *pagan* false prophets who crept in, *that the Holy Spirit is a Third Person*—the *heresy of the "trinity."* This limits God to "Three Persons." This *denies* that Christ, through His Holy Spirit actually comes now *into* the converted Christian and does His saving work on the *inside*—"Christ in you, the hope of glory" (Colossians 1:27).

Jesus Christ is *come* in the flesh, as inspired in its original Greek language means, literally, *present tense*—that *Christ is now coming.* . . .

. . .If the Holy Spirit were a third *person* that would be impossible!

. . .That heresy *denies* the *true born-again* experience![38]

V. *Salvation by Grace and Law*

Salvation, then, is a *process!*

But how the god of this world would blind your eyes to that! He tries to deceive you into thinking all there is to it is just "accepting Christ" with *"no works"*—and presto-chango, you are pronounced "Saved."

But the *Bible* reveals that *none* is yet "saved."[39]

The *blood* of Christ does not finally save any man. The death of Christ merely paid the penalty of sin in our stead—it wipes the slate clean of past sins—it saves us merely from the *death penalty*—it removes that which separated us from God and reconciles us to God.

---

[36]*The Plain Truth*, April 1963, p. 10.
[37]Herbert W. Armstrong, *What Do You Mean—Salvation?*, Pasadena, CA: Ambassador Press, n.d., p. 19.
[38]*Just What Do You Mean Born Again?*, *op. cit.*, p. 13.
[39]*Why Were You Born?*, *op. cit.*, p. 11.

But we are *saved*—that is, given immortal life—by Christ's *life*, not by His death (Romans 5:10).

It is *only those* who, during this Christian, Spirit-begotten life, have grown in knowledge and grace, have overcome, have developed spiritually, done the works of Christ, and endured unto the end, who shall finally be given *immortality*—finally changed from mortal to *immortal* at the time of the Second Coming of Christ (1 Corinthians 15:53, 54).[40]

People have been taught, falsely, that "Christ *completed* the plan of salvation on the Cross"—when actually it was only *begun* there. The popular denominations have taught, "Just *believe*— that's all there is to it; believe on the Lord Jesus Christ, and you are that instant *saved!*"

That teaching is false! And because of deception—because the *true Gospel* of Jesus Christ has been all but blotted out, lo these 1900 years by the preaching of a false gospel *about [the] person* of Christ—and often a false Christ at that—millions today *worship Christ—and all in vain!*

The blood of Christ does not finally save any man. The death of Christ did pay the penalty of sin in our stead—it wipes the slate clean of past sins—it saves us merely from the *death penalty*—it removes that which separated us from God and reconciles us to God.[41]

. . . So it is not only *possible* but obligatory—that we obey God's spiritual law, the *ten commandments*, as they are magnified throughout the Bible. Keeping them in the spirit does *not mean* "spiritualizing" them away.

. . . But by exercising the *will* to always obey God, and by receiving the extra help He needed to master His fleshly desires, Jesus *repudiated* the sway of sin of the human flesh and showed that the law of God *could be kept.*[42]

VI. *The New Birth and the Resurrection*

But, He was then *born [of God], how?* By a resurrection from the dead (Romans 1:4). *When? At the time* of His resurrection!

And *that is* the way *you* and I shall look, if and when we are finally *born [of God]!* These deceived people who talk about having had a "born again experience" certainly don't look like *that!*

That tremendous, glorious event of being *born of God* is to take place *at the resurrection of the just*— at the time of Christ's Second Coming to earth![43]

It is *only* those who, during this Christian, Spirit-begotten life, have grown in knowledge and grace, have overcome, have

---

[40]Herbert W. Armstrong, *All About Water Baptism*, Pasadena, CA: Ambassador Press, n.d., pp. 1-3.

[41]*All About Water Baptism, op. cit.*, p. 6.

[42]*The Plain Truth*, November 1963, pp. 11, 12.

[43]*Just What Do You Mean Born Again?, op. cit.*, p. 13.

29

developed spiritually, done the works of Christ, and endured unto the end, who shall finally be given *immortality*—finally changed from mortal to *immortal* at the time of the Second Coming of Christ (1 Corinthians 15:53-54).[44]

The real *source of this whole stupendous error* is this. In the English language, we have *two different* words to express the *two phases* that occur in the reproductive process of all mammals.

The one, which is the very Start of the new life, we call *conception*, or a *begettal*.

But *no one ever calls this beginning of the process a* birth!

The phase of the process which in the English language we call being *born* is that process by which the foetus is *delivered* from the mother's womb, and out into the world comes a little baby to gasp its own first breath. It has then *been born!*

But if you would try to tell a doctor, or a nurse, that the yet unborn foetus has already been *born*, as soon as you knew it had been *conceived*, or *begotten*, the doctor or nurse would surely think you ignorant, and probably try to explain.

The New Testament of the Holy Bible was originally written in the *Greek* language. And, in this case, the Greeks had *only one word* for the *two* vitally *different* phases of the process!

That Greek word is "gennao"(pronounced ghen-ah-o). The Greek-English dictionary (lexicon) gives this definition of the Greek word; *to procreate* (properly of the father, but by extension of the mother): beget, be born, bring forth, conceive, be delivered of, gender.

Four of those definitions mean to beget or to conceive—but *not* to be *born*. To *procreate means to beget*. To *conceive* has the same meaning. Webster's dictionary defines "gender" as to beget, breed, generate. It does *not refer* to the birth. But three of the Lexicon definitions of "gennao" mean the actual *birth*: "be born," "bring forth" and "be delivered of."

. . . and since the "scholars" of our comparatively recent years who translated the Bible into English did not, themselves, *understand* God's Plan—they often translate the Greek word "gennao" into the English word "*born*" where it actually meant "begotten."

". . . for in Christ Jesus I have *begotten* you through the gospel." There it is correctly translated, showing that Paul's converts at Corinth, as his "spiritual children," had been *begotten* of God, *but not yet born.*

The experience of conversion, in this life, is a *begettal*—a "conception—an impregnation"—but *not yet a birth*. This we shall make *plain*.

All who *now* are *begotten* sons of God shall then be *born*—elevated from mortal to *immortal*, from decaying *flesh* to *spirit*,

---

[44]*All About Water Baptism*, pp. 1, 3.

from *human to divine!* And that *true born-again experience* will be as incomparably more *glorious* than the fake, vague, meaningless, so-called "born-again experience" that deceived *thousands think* they have had, now, as the present transcending *glory of Christ* is superior to the status of sickly, diseased, sinning, suffering *humanity today!*[45]

. . . After people are actually *born of God*, they, too, shall *be spirit, just as* God is Spirit. They will be invisible to material human sight, just as angels are.

He is now *begotten* of God. The very *life* and *nature* of God has *entered into* him, impregnating him with immortal spirit—life, exactly as the physical sperm cell from the human father enters into the ovum or physical egg-cell when a new *human life* is first *conceived, impregnated, or begotten.* But, just as that tiny ovum, as small as a pin-point, is merely *begotten* of its human father—*not yet born*—so the converted human is, at what we properly call, conversion, merely *begotten* of God the heavenly Father—*not yet born.*

He is *still* material *flesh,* even though God's Spirit has now *entered into* his *mind.* He is *still visible.*

A newly converted human is actually *begotten of* God. Such a person is, already, an actual begotten *son of God.* He can call God "Father." *But He is Not Yet Born of God.*[46]

All true Christians who shall have died before Christ's coming shall rise first—in a resurrection—and then all Christians *still alive,* in mortal flesh, shall be instantaneously—in the twinkling of an eye—*changed from mortal to immortal*—from material flesh to immaterial spirit—from *human* to *divine,* at last *born of God!*

We are now *flesh*—vile, corruptible flesh subject to rotting and decay. But at Christ's coming, when we shall be *born of God,* this vile body shall be *changed,* and made exactly like Jesus in His *glorified body.*[47]

VII. *The Guilt of God and the Nature of Man*

God has *made* man's natural mind so that it wants to do things that are contrary to His laws; "The carnal mind (with which we are all born) is enmity against God" (Romans 8:7). Compare this with Romans 3:9–18. "The flesh (man's natural heart and mind) *lusteth* against the Spirit and the Spirit against the flesh: and these are *contrary* the one to the other" (Galatians 5:17). *All,* as originally born, have a desire-lust—to go contrary to God's Laws! (James 1:4 and Psalm 81:11, 12).

It *is by man's own carnal mind that God blinds him* . . .

[45]*Just What Do You Mean Born Again?* pages 6, 18, 19, 20.
[46]*Ibid.*, p. 11.
[47]*Ibid.*, pp. 13-15.

God, in love and wisdom, blinds human beings who by nature reject the truth so they will unwittingly *sin all the more often* and thereby *learn their lesson all the more deeply.*[48]

VIII. *The Sabbath, Unclean Foods and Legalism*—1 Timothy 4:4
Passover, the days of unleavened bread, Pentecost, and the holy days God had ordained *forever* were all observed by Jesus . . .
The New Testament reveals that Jesus, the apostles, and the New Testament Church, both Jewish and Gentile-born, observed God's Sabbath, and God's festivals—weekly and annually.[49]

The Theology of Biblical Christianity

In the tradition of Jehovah's Witnesses whom he follows concerning the doctrine of eternal retribution and the Resurrection of Jesus Christ, Herbert Armstrong's theology has no room for the deity or personality of the Holy Spirit.

For Armstrong, God's Holy Spirit is an impersonal "it," and though he makes a pathetic effort to rescue the divinity of the Spirit, he only succeeds in reducing Him to "the love of God" on abstract principle at best.

In our analysis of the theology of Jehovah's Witnesses we observed how the depersonalization of the Holy Spirit strikes at the very heart of the Christian Gospel, for it is through the agency of the third person of the Trinity that God regenerates men to eternal life (John 3:5). By denying the personality of the Spirit, i.e., that the Spirit is a personal ego and one of the persons of the Holy Trinity, Armstrong invalidates the only means whereby a man can be saved. All too few listeners to his program are aware of this particular serious deviation from historic Christianity. It is always wise to keep in mind that the more vigorously they enunciate what small fragments of truth that somehow manage to escape the multiple strands of error woven into the very fabric of the The Worldwide Church of God, the more carefully one ought to listen for the inevitable overtones of Armstrong's interpretations which nullify the small percentage of truth he does retain.

It is unnecessary to repeat what we have stated before, but even a careful consideration of the thirteenth chapter of Acts reveals that the Holy Spirit uses the personal pronoun "I," denoting

---

[48]C. P. Meredith, *Is This the Only Day of Salvation?*, Pasadena, CA: Ambassador Press, n.d., p. 2.
[49]Herbert W. Armstrong, *Easter Is Pagan*, Pasadena, CA: Ambassador Press, n.d., pp. 4, 12.

ego or personality. He also commands the Church to set apart Paul and Barnabas, then He sends them forth (verses 2 through 4).

The twenty-first chapter of the Book of Acts pictures the Spirit instructing the prophet, Agabus, to speak: "Thus says the Holy Spirit, So shall the Jews at Jerusalem bind the man that owns this belt, and shall deliver him into the hands of the Gentiles" (verse 11).

Thus Luke reveals that the third person of the Trinity has the capacity to think, command and prophesy. This certainly does not correspond to Mr. Armstrong's caricature of the Spirit as an "it." For even an elementary knowledge of psychology reveals that an "it" is devoid of personality and cannot speak, command or prophesy!

Further analysis of the fifth chapter of Acts underscores that the Holy Spirit is deity and is so designated by the Apostle Paul (verses 3 and 4). That the Holy Spirit is considered a member of the heavenly Trinity is evident by His presence at the incarnation (Luke 1:35), the baptism of Christ (Matthew 3:16), the Resurrection of Christ (Romans 8:11 and 1 Peter 3:18), and in the Great Commission (Matthew 28:19).

One cannot read Mr. Armstrong's writings without becoming increasingly aware of the fact that he is radically anti-Trinitarian. A perusal of the quotation from his writings found in the earlier part of this chapter indicates forcefully that he wants no part of Christian theology in this and far too many other areas for the spiritual good of himself or his listeners.

In the theology of Herbert Armstrong:

> Genesis 1:1 gives God's name as in the Hebrew Elohim. This is a uniplural name. It means more than one person, but combined into the family, which family is God. . . . For the word "God" comes to us from the Hebrew word "Elohim" which means "living, eternal, creating, all-powerful, governing kingdom." Elohim means one God, not many gods. But that one God is a kingdom. There is but one true church—one church but many members! (1 Corinthians 12:20). So it is with God.
>
> Do you really grasp it? The purpose of your being alive is that finally you will be born into the kingdom of God when *you will actually be God* even as Jesus was and is God and His Father a different person also is God! . . . You are setting out on a training to become Creator, to become God![50]

The similarity to Mormonism in Armstrong's theology at this

---

[50]*Just What Do You Mean Born Again?*, op. cit., pp. 16-20.

point is quite striking, for as previously observed in our chapter on the Mormons, they, too, believe and teach that men may become members of the God-family and become gods. Armstrong, on the other hand, exceeds even the Mormon fantasy, boldly teaching what appears to be a pantheistic unity of God in which all the members of the "family" participate. This is certainly a view which is not shared by any of the inspired writers of the Scripture, and his recourse to the Hebrew plural (Elohim) in which he stretches it beyond all proportion and contextual meaning to the forced interpretation of a "family" or "kingdom," is indirectly a pathetic admission of the extremely limited knowledge he possesses of the language.

Armstrong's usage of Elohim is not consistent with any scholarly presentation; in fact, as he uses it, it is simply a perversion tailored to impress those who can be impressed with the ludicrous.

The followers of Armstrong's cult should consult the third chapter of Genesis where they will find that Satan first taught the "God family" doctrine to Adam and Eve. Both Armstrong and the Mormons have received and believed the same perversion which ushered in the reign of sin and death upon the human race, for if Satan lied when he said "you shall be as gods" (verse 5), so does Mr. Armstrong "wrest the Scripture to his own destruction" and sadly to the destruction, spiritually speaking, of those who follow in his training.

The plain truth of this whole matter is that we do indeed grasp what Mr. Armstrong is teaching. His Worldwide Church of God serves only as a camouflage for his doctrinal deviations which are mixed with orthodox terminology and evangelical clichés and infused with numerous half-truths. This concoction is enunciated with a dogmatism and arrogance akin to that of the late Judge Rutherford of Jehovah's Witnesses. And were it not for Armstrong's dynamic presentation and wide media coverage coupled with the spiritual vacuum which today pervades many quarters of Christendom, his entire system of interpretation would be the object of humor instead of the serious consideration it now demands.

The Armstrong cult appeals to the Hebrew and Greek languages and is conspicuously devoid of the scholastic background or knowledge of the languages which Armstrong so glibly quotes. The Hebrew plural Elohim, as we have stated, does not refer to any family or kingdom of God; it is one of the divine names utilized in Scripture and is distorted by the Mormons, Jehovah's Witnesses and Mr. Armstrong in a vain attempt to alter the nature of God which, as revealed in the Bible, controverts their respective theologies.

In our study of Jehovah's Witnesses the doctrine of the Trinity has been given full consideration, so it will not be necessary to go into further detail on this subject. But it should not be forgotten that every major non-Christian cult system either perverts subtly or denies outright the Christian doctrine of the Trinity; and Mr. Armstrong's cult is no exception to the rule, even though he mixes the theologies of Jehovah's Witnesses and Mormonism with his own peculiar interpretations. The denial is uniquely his own and should be recognized for what it is.

The New Birth—A New Twist

The doctrine of the New Birth or Spiritual Regeneration as it is taught in the New Testament apparently has an effect upon Mr. Armstrong when he either hears or reads it which is little short of hysterical. In his pamphlet, *Just What Do You Mean Born Again* he vigorously criticizes the Christian doctrine of regeneration, and in its place substitutes by all odds, one of the strangest doctrines in the area of cultism. Through it he has quite literally given the new birth a new twist!

According to the theology of The Worldwide Church of God, the doctrine of the new birth is divided into two segments or areas. In the first or initial area which takes place upon the acceptance of Jesus Christ as the Son of God, the believer is impregnated with the life of God through the Holy Spirit which Armstrong terms "begetting." The second phase is the new birth itself which he informs us takes place not at the moment of faith but at the resurrection of the body!

Mr. Armstrong strenuously maintains that it is "a universal error" to believe that when a person is converted and has fully repented and accepted Christ in faith that that person is born again in the Biblical sense. For Herbert Armstrong the original Greek word *Gennao* is the pivot point of the controversy. Armstrong holds that since the word can also be translated "beget" or "conceive," the translators of the Bible erred in not rendering the word consistently as "begotten" instead of "born," and this they did because "they did not themselves understand God's plan . . . the experience of conversion in this life in a begettal, a conception, an impregnation, but not yet a birth."

It is worthwhile to note in studying this particular phase of Mr. Armstrong's theology that his appeal to the Greek, which was meant by him to carry the convincing weight of scholastic authority, in reality becomes the proverbial albatross around his neck. Mr. Armstrong's contention that "the original Greek in which the New Testament was written has only the one word for both meanings" is a most damaging remark, for any good lexicon reveals immediately that the Greek has at least four other terms to describe the idea of conception and birth (*sullabousa, tiktei, apotelestheisa,* and *apokuei*) which are translated variously as "conceive," "bring forth," "delivered," "born," "when finished," and "begat." One need only study Luke 1:24, 37; 2:21, 36; James 1:15, 18 and not a few others, and he will come to the immediate conclusion that Mr. Armstrong has no concept whatever of New Testament Greek. In fact, the Greek language even has a term which describes pregnancy from conception to delivery!

Mr. Armstrong's blatant statement to the effect that "the Greek had only one word for two vitally different phases of the process . . . since the original Greek in which the New Testament was written had only the one word for both meanings (*gennao*)," is either a product of his own ignorance or a deliberate falsehood. Since he seems to be aware of the existence of lexicons and concordances, this writer is convinced that it is the latter.

It is only necessary to look for a moment at Mr. Armstrong's manufactured distinction between the uses of *gennao* in the New Testament to see that his attempt to stretch the term beyond all limits of its usage in New Testament Greek, is only done in order to teach that no one is *now* born again of the Holy Spirit, but that instead this can only take place at the resurrection.

The followers of Mr. Armstrong must settle for an impregnation by the Spirit and a gestation period (their entire life!) before they can be born again. This new birth is dependent upon keeping the commandments of God and enduring to the end in Mr. Armstrong's theology, a fact overlooked by some of his more zealous disciples.

The fact that the new birth has nothing to do with the resurrection is demonstrated by the usage of the term by the Apostle Peter who reminds us that through faith in the Lord Jesus Christ we have been "born again (past tense) not of corruptible seed, but of incorruptible, by the Word of God which liveth and abideth forever" (1 Peter 1:23).

The new birth in the New Testament is synonymous with spiritual regeneration to eternal life, and the very fact that Jesus Christ and the apostles described the possessors of the new birth as "saved" decimates Mr. Armstrong's contention that one must wait until the resurrection in order to be born again.

In his epistle to the Ephesians the Apostle Paul is adamant in his declaration that "by grace you have been saved through faith; and this is not your own doing, it is the gift of God—not because of works, lest any one should boast" (Ephesians 2:8, Greek). Here is the usage of the past tense in reference to Christians, an instance which is amply supplemented throughout the New Testament by such passages as John 5:24; 3:36; 6:47; Romans 8:1; 1 Peter 1:18 and 1 John 5:1, 11-13 and 20.

It is wholly unnecessary to pursue this thought further since Mr. Armstrong has no scholarly precedent for subdividing the new birth and attempting to attach it to the resurrection of the body, something which the Scripture nowhere does. His is a lame attempt to distort the basic meaning of *gennao* which he, himself, admits is listed in the lexicon as "to be born, to bring forth, to be delivered of." It is only one more indication of the limitations of his resources.

When Jesus Christ addressed Nicodemus (John 3) and spoke of the new birth, He connected this birth to the person of the Holy Spirit whom the disciples received in the Upper Room (John 20) and whose power and presence were manifested at Pentecost (Acts 2). This has always been accepted in Christian theology for just what the Bible says it is, an instantaneous experience of spiritual cleansing and re-creation synonymous with the exercise of saving faith in the person of Jesus Christ and through the agency of the grace of God (Acts 16:31; 2:8–10; Colossians 1:13, 14; Galatians 2:20; 1 Corinthians 6:11, 19; 2 Corinthians 5:17).

The Apostle Paul instructs us that our salvation has been accomplished not by any efforts on our part, but by "the kindness and love of God our Savior" (Titus 3:4-7). It is not something we must wait for until the resurrection; it is our present possession in Christ totally separate from the immortality of the body which is to be bestowed at the return of Christ and the resurrection of the body (1 Corinthians 15:49–54; 1 John 3:2; Romans 6:5).

It is all well and good if Mr. Armstrong's followers wish to make the new birth a process, as indeed they do with the doctrine of salvation, but we must be quick to point out that this is not the Christian doctrine of the new birth and as such is not consistent with the revelation of the Bible. Mr. Armstrong's new twist to the new birth is just that, and the Christian Church can ill afford to sit by in silence while The Worldwide Church of God propagates it as Biblical theology.

The Resurrection of Christ

The Resurrection of Jesus Christ along with the Christian doctrine of the Trinity is assailed most vigorously by the majority of non-Christian religious cultists. Such persons steadfastly maintain that they believe in the Resurrection of Christ, but then proceed to redefine the term "resurrection" until it generally comes to mean merely the conquest of death by the spiritual nature of Jesus. Herbert Armstrong is no exception in this category, teaching as he does that Jesus Christ was raised from the dead as a spirit and that the saints will be resurrected as spirits.

Wrote Mr. Armstrong:

The saints of God now born of the spirit and become spirit at the resurrection will be able to be invisible or visible at will.[51]

The Worldwide Church of God does not hesitate to state that "the resurrected body was no longer human. . . ." and that Jesus Christ Himself was spirit in His Resurrection:

Now notice carefully God the Father did not cause Jesus Christ to get back into the body which had died. Nowhere does the Scripture say He was alive and active or that God had Him get back into the human body that had died and was now resurrected . . . and the resurrected body was no longer human . . . He was again changed and converted into immortality . . .[52]

What has been said about Jehovah's Witnesses' doctrine of the Resurrection of Christ can also be said about Armstrong's position.

The reader can consult the second chapter of John's gospel (verses 19–21) to ascertain from the lips of the Lord Jesus that He promised to raise His own body from the grave. The Greek word as has been observed (*soma*) refers to a physical form not to an immortal spirit!

Luke goes to great pains to point out that Christ identified the body in which He conquered death as physical in nature (flesh and bone), and further that this body had the marks of the cross in the hands and feet (Luke 24:37–39).

---

[51]*The Plain Truth*, October 1959, p. 30.
[52]*The Plain Truth*, April 1963, pp. 10, 40.

The Apostle Thomas could not doubt that Christ had risen in the physical form after our Lord's appearance in the Upper Room (see John 20), for it was there that the risen Christ invited him to place his fingers into the wounds in His hand and his hand into the spear wound in His side. One thing is certain from all this, Jesus Christ conquered death *as a man not* as a spirit, and at this juncture Mr. Armstrong's theology is in complete opposition to the revelation of the Scripture. At the Second Coming of Christ (1 Thessalonians 4) when the dead in Christ rise, they will rise immortal according to the Apostle Paul (1 Corinthians 15) and will possess a form like Christ's own form (1 John 3:2). This form will be composed of flesh and bone in the structural composition of Christ's resurrected body (Luke 24), for nowhere does the Bible say that either Christ or the resurrected bodies of Christians are composed of spirit.

In the 26th chapter of Matthew's gospel, Jesus Christ promised His disciples that they would drink wine with Him in the kingdom of His Father (verse 29), and He reiterated this same promise in Luke's gospel, "you may eat and drink at my table in my kingdom" (Luke 22:30).

It is the hope of Christians that at His glorious appearing Jesus Christ will "change our vile body that it may be fashioned like unto His own glorious body" (Philippians 3:21). And if He is indeed the firstfruits of them that slept (1 Corinthians 15:20), then we shall indeed be like Him (1 John 3:2); and He is an immortal man, not a spirit as Mr. Armstrong's theology so erroneously declares.

Salvation and Atonement

As the theology to The Worldwide Church of God does violence to the true nature of the new birth, so also does it categorically deny the Biblical doctrine of the Atonement.

According to Mr. Armstrong:

> Salvation then is a process but how the god of this world would blind your eyes to that! He tries to deceive you into thinking all there is to it is just accepting Christ with no works, and presto changeover, you are pronounced saved! . . . But the Bible reveals that none is as yet saved . . . people have been taught falsely that Christ completed the plan of salvation on the cross when actually it was only begun there. The popular denominations have taught just believe that's all there is to it, believe on the Lord Jesus Christ and you are that instant saved. That teaching is false . . . the blood of Christ does not finally save any man, the death of Christ merely

paid the penalty of sin in our stead and wipes the slate clean of *past* sins ... it is only those who during this Christian spirit-begotten life have grown in knowledge and grace, have overcome, have developed spiritually, done the works of Christ and endured to the end who shall finally be given immortality, finally changed from mortal to immortal, at the time of the Second Coming of Christ. So being, as we say, converted, receiving the Holy Spirit of God is merely the beginning! Then begins a life long of living under the government of God by God's laws which expresses His will instead of by self-will and desire.[53]

After reading Mr. Armstrong's statements, any serious student of the Bible wonders how anyone could take seriously his theological interpretations, for if there is one thing that the Bible does emphatically teach, it is the fact that salvation is *not* a process but an accomplished fact based upon the completed sacrifice of Jesus Christ (Hebrews 1:3; 9:26, 28).

Regarding Mr. Armstrong's shocking statement to the effect that the blood of Christ does not finally save anyone, it is in direct contradiction to the words of the Apostle Peter who taught that persons have not been redeemed by anything corruptible but "by the precious blood of Christ" (1 Peter 1:19). It should be noted that this is the *past tense* as an accomplished fact, a teaching amplified in the Book of Hebrews repeatedly. The writer of Hebrews tells us that "by one offering He has perfected forever them that are sanctified" and that by the will of God "we are sanctified through the offering of the body of Jesus Christ once for all" (Hebrews 10:14, 20).

The Lord Jesus has entered

not into a sanctuary made with hands, a copy of the true one, but into heaven itself, now to appear in the presence of God on our behalf. ... But as it is, he has appeared once for all of the end of the age to put away sin by the sacrifice of himself. And just as it is appointed for men to die once, and after that comes judgment, so Christ, having been offered once to bear the sins of many, will appear a second time, not to deal with sin but to save those who are eagerly waiting for him (Hebrews 9:24–28, RSV).

Mr. Armstrong and his Worldwide Church of God consistently ignore the fact that

Christ had offered for all time a single sacrifice for sins. Therefore, brethren since we ... have confidence to enter the sanctuary by the blood of Jesus, by the new and living way which he opened

---

[53]*Why Were You Born?*, p. 11.

for us through the curtain, that is, through his flesh, and since we have a greater priest over the house of God, let us draw near with a true heart in full assurance of faith, with our hearts sprinkled clean from an evil conscience and our bodies washed with pure water. Let us hold fast the confession of our hope without wavering, for he who promised is faithful (Hebrews 10:12–23, RSV).

The Apostle Paul reiterates the completed nature of the atonement upon the cross when he deals with the subject in such passages as Ephesians 1:7, Colossians 1:20 and Romans 5:9. The Apostle John's reminder that God has provided for continual cleansing from sin (1 John 1:7, 9) should only serve to strengthen Christians in the knowledge that Jesus Christ has indeed by the sacrifice of the cross "loosed us from our sins in His own blood" (Revelation 1:5, Greek). This is a completed act, the benefits of which are shed abroad in the hearts of all true believers by the Holy Spirit. Nowhere does the Bible teach that the atonement of Christ is *yet* to be completed! This particular doctrine is drawn from the early writings of Seventh-day Adventists with whom, as we mentioned, Mr. Armstrong was associated at one time. It is to the credit of the Adventists that their denomination has officially repudiated this position, maintaining that the atonement has already been completed.

Pauline theology makes clear the fact that in Jesus Christ God has determined to redeem men by sovereign grace, and the record still stands:

For what saith the scripture? Abraham believed God, and it was counted unto him for righteousness. Now to him that worketh is the reward not reckoned of grace, but of debt. But to him that worketh not, but believeth on him that justifieth the ungodly, his faith is counted for righteousness. Even as David also describeth the blessedness of the man, unto whom God imputeth righteousness without works, Saying, blessed are they whose iniquities are forgiven, and whose sins are covered. Blessed is the man to whom the Lord will not impute sin (Romans 4:3–8).

The theology of The Worldwide Church of God in regard to the doctrine of salvation is refuted thoroughly by the Apostle Paul in his epistle to the Galatians. When describing the purpose of the law of God, Paul points out that its primary function was to "lead us to Christ" that we might be justified by faith. The law was a pedagogue, a teacher, but it was finally and completely fulfilled in the person of the incarnate Jesus Christ. Love is the universal, all fulfilling principle which is implemented through grace, first toward God and then toward one's neighbor. (See Romans 13:8–11.)

Mr. Armstrong attaches to salvation the requirement of "keeping the law and commandments of God." This can only be described as adding to the gospel of grace the condition of law-keeping, a first century heresy scathingly denounced in the Galatian epistle as "another gospel" by no less an authority on the law than St. Paul (Galatians 2:16, 21; 1:8, 9).

If all law is fulfilled in love as Christ and the apostles taught, then the insistence upon observance of the Ten Commandments (or, for that matter, the over six hundred laws of Moses) on the part of Mr. Armstrong and his followers as a condition of salvation injects into the Christian Church what the apostles so successfully expelled (Matthew 22:36-40; Acts 15:24).

It is certainly true that no informed Christian believes in the destruction or setting aside of the laws of God, but, as we shall see, when dealing with the Seventh-day Adventists' concept of this subject, there is a vast difference between the abolition of law and the fulfillment of law, which fulfillment Christ accomplished once for all on the cross (Romans 3:31; 10:4).

The theology of Herbert Armstrong includes what can only be termed a type of universalism where the redemption of man is concerned:

> As Lord of lords Christ will begin to convert and save the entire world during His reign . . . all peoples will then come to know God. Their blindness and religious confusion will be removed and they will finally be converted. The resurrected saints will teach the people God's way.[54]

The New Testament repeatedly urges men to assume the forgiveness God has provided now, not during some future millennial reign. "Now is the accepted time; behold, now is the day of salvation" (2 Corinthians 6:2), is the watchword of the New Testament theology. Along with "Pastor" Russell, the founder of Jehovah's Witnesses, Armstrong teaches what amounts to a second chance for unregenerate men.

Jesus Christ urged men to accept Him "for the Son of man is come to seek and to save that which was lost" (Luke 19:9, 10) and the writer of Hebrews emphasizes "how shall we escape if we neglect so great salvation" (Hebrews 2:3).

The writer of Hebrews also exploded another of Mr. Arm-

---

[54]*The Plain Truth*, October 1959, p. 30.

strong's theological fantasies when he wrote that during the millennial kingdom "they shall not teach every man his neighbor, and every man his brother, saying, Know the Lord: for all shall know me, from the least to the greatest" (Hebrews 8:11). The followers of The Worldwide Church of God would do well to put Mr. Armstrong's theology to the test (1 Thessalonians 5:21), for then it would be apparent that what he says is anything but "the plain truth."

Inherent within the theological structure of The Worldwide Church of God and stemming from Mr. Armstrong's perversion of the Biblical doctrine of salvation, is his insistence (also borrowed from the Seventh-day Adventist) that Christians abstain from specific types of food which he claims are "unclean."

No devoted follower of The Worldwide Church will therefore eat pork, lobster, clams, shrimp or oysters or any of the prohibitions of the Mosaic system. They are in effect Orthodox Jews in this particular area of theology!

In his first epistle to Timothy the Apostle Paul recognized among the Gentiles the problem of so-called unclean foods and dealt with it in the following manner:

> Now the Spirit expressly says that in later times some will depart from the faith by giving heed to deceitful spirits and doctrines of demons, through the pretensions of liars whose consciences are seared, who forbid marriage and enjoin abstinence from foods which God created to be received with thanksgiving by those who believe and know the truth. For everything created by God is good, and nothing is to be rejected if it is received with thanksgiving; for then it is consecrated by the word of God and prayer (1Timothy 4:1–5, RSV).

Further comment on this particular subject is unnecessary in the light of the Apostle's clear statement, but a reading of the fourteenth chapter of Romans reveals instantly that Christians are not to sit in judgment upon one another relative to days of worship or foods to be consumed. We are not to judge spirituality on the basis of diet or the observance of days. But in The Worldwide Church of God this is not true, for Mr. Armstrong does indeed sit in judgment upon all those who do not subscribe to his particular interpretation of dietary laws allegedly enforced in this era of history.

Relative to the problem of Sabbath-keeping, Mr. Armstrong also derived this from the Seventh-day Adventist denomination, but he has gone further than the Adventist have ever even intimated.

The literature of The Worldwide Church of God is literally filled with insistence upon the observance of the Jewish feast days, new moons, festivals and sabbaths, all of which were dealt with fully and finally by the Apostle Paul in his Colossian epistle.

> And you who were dead in trespasses and the uncircumcision of your flesh, God made alive together with him, having forgiven all our trespasses, having canceled the bond which stood against us with its legal demands; this he set aside, nailing it to the cross. He disarmed the principalities and powers and made a public example of them, triumphing over them in him. Therefore, let no one pass judgment on you in question of food and drink or with regard to a festival, a new moon or a sabbath. These are only a shadow of what is to come; but the substance belongs to Christ (2:13–17, RSV).

When the preceding quotation from Paul is placed beside his counsel in Romans 14, the picture is transparently clear:

> Let not him who eats despise him who abstains, and let not him who abstains pass judgment on him who eats; for God has welcomed him. Who are you to pass judgment on the servant of another? It is before his own master that he stands or falls. And he will be upheld for the Master is able to make him stand. One man esteems one day as better than another, while another man esteems all days alike. Let everyone be fully convinced in his own mind. He who observes the day, observes it in honor of the Lord. He also who eats, eats in honor of the Lord, since he gives thanks to God; while he who abstains, abstains in honor of the Lord and gives thanks to God. . . . Why do you pass judgment on your brother? Or you, why do you despise your brother? . . . Then let us no more pass judgment on one another, but rather decide never to put a stumbling-block or hindrance in the way of a brother. I know and am persuaded in the Lord Jesus that nothing is unclean in itself; but it is unclean for anyone who thinks it unclean. . . . Do not, for the sake of food, destroy the work of God. Everything is indeed clean, but it is wrong for anyone to make others fall by what he eats; it is right not to eat meat or drink wine or do anything that makes your brother stumble (14:3–21, RSV).

There is a memorable passage in the Book of Acts where the Council of Jerusalem was in session concerning the problem of Jewish prohibitions on diet and practice as it affected the Gentile converts. Apostle James once for all time dealt with the issue, a fact Mr. Armstrong seems content to ignore:

> Therefore my sentence is, that we trouble not them, which from among the Gentiles are turned to God; But that we write unto them, that they abstain from pollutions of idols, and from

fornication, and from things strangled, and from blood . . . For-
asmuch as we have heard, that certain which went out from us
have troubled you with words, subverting your souls, saying, Ye
must be circumcised and keep the law: to whom we gave no such
commandment. . . . For it seemed good to the Holy Ghost, and to
us, to lay upon you no greater burden than these necessary things;
that you abstain from meats offered to idols, and from blood, and
from things strangled, and from fornication: from which if ye keep
yourselves, ye shall do well (Acts 15:19, 20, 24–29).

It is evident that law keeping, dietary prohibitions, the Mosaic
ordinances which were binding upon Israel, and the Jewish cus-
toms of observances of feasts, etc., were abrogated by the Holy
Spirit (verse 28), and it is certainly not amiss to comment that
what the Spirit of God saw fit to lift as restrictions upon the Church
of Jesus Christ, the so-called Worldwide Church of God has no
right to reimpose! Mr. Armstrong, however, has done precisely this
and his action stands condemned not only by the Council at Jerusalem and the Apostle James but by the clear words of the
Apostle Paul and the pronouncement of the Holy Spirit Himself.

The Indictment of God

We close our observations on the theology of the Armstrong
cult by pointing out that he has not hesitated to indict God for the
guilt of man.

> God has made man's natural mind so that it wants to do things
> that are contrary to His laws . . . it is by man's own carnal mind
> that God blinds him . . . God in love and wisdom blinds human
> beings who by nature reject the truth so they will unwittingly sin
> all the more often and thereby learn their lesson all the more
> deeply . . .[55]

While it is certainly true that the carnal mind "is enmity
against God" (Romans 8:7) and that "the natural man does not
receive the things of the Spirit" and by nature rebels against the
decrees of the Creator, nowhere in Scripture does it state that God
"made man's natural mind so that it wants to do things contrary
to His laws," as Mr. Armstrong's theology teaches. Rather, it is
the clear testimony of Scripture that each member of the human
race has chosen to voluntarily and freely rebel against the Lord,
thereby, coming into possession of carnal or fleshly natures which
are at enmity with God.

---

[55]*Is This the Only Day of Salvation?*, p. 2.

The fifth chapter of Romans informs us that the spiritual attributes of rebellion are in all men because of Adam's disobedience and that only in Christ can these be changed by the creation of a new nature, thus restoring man to fellowship with God.

In the theology of Mr. Armstrong's cult, then, God is ultimately responsible for the evil nature of man, and he has not even hesitated to state concerning the human nature and character of the Lord Jesus Christ:

> Christ now had become human having human nature with all of its desires, weaknesses and lusts . . . and subject to death just like any other human. This is a truth about which millions are deceived.[56]

When dealing with the sinless nature and character of Christ, Mr. Armstrong states:

> . . .He was the first human ever to achieve it—to be perfected, finished as a perfect character.[57]

In the fifteenth chapter of 1 Corinthians the Apostle Paul contradicts Mr. Armstrong in the strongest possible terms by referring to Jesus Christ as "the last Adam," (verse 45) thereby teaching incontrovertibly that Jesus Christ had a perfect human nature and character and was never under obligation to achieve it or "to be perfected, finished as a perfect character." He was perfect as the last Adam and as the eternal Word made flesh (John 1:1, 14).

It is perfectly true that the Scriptures speak of Christ as "learning obedience as a faithful son." It is also true that He was made "complete" (Hebrews 2:10; 5:9; 7:28). The Greek word translated "perfect" in the passages from Hebrews basically means "completion," a fact demonstrated by Jesus Christ Himself when in speaking of Herod, He said:

"And He said unto them, go ye and tell that fox, Behold, I cast out devils, and I do cures today and tomorrow, and the third day I shall be perfected" (Luke 13:32).

The Revised Standard Version correctly renders the word "finish," carrying with it the meaning of the completion of a plan, literally "I finish my course." Far from being imperfect and in need of suffering and death to perfect His character and human nature as Armstrong maintains, these terms only describe the completion of the divine plan of the ages whereby God brought to

---

[56]*The Plain Truth*, November 1963, pp. 11, 12.
[57]*Why Were You Born?* p. 14.

completion or fulfillment the foreordained consummation of His majestic design for human redemption. The attempt by Mr. Armstrong to imbue Jesus Christ with a tainted human nature and to seize upon the word "perfect" as the means to accomplish this, cannot alter the plain declarations of Scripture which describe our Lord in His human nature and character in far different terms than does Mr. Armstrong. When applied to our Lord, the term "perfect" or "perfected" refers only to Christ's completion of His human life and sacrifice for our sins. He became complete only in the sense of perfect obedience and submission to the Father's will. He was always "holy" and without sin in His human nature and character.

In the gospel of Luke which describes the annunciation to the virgin Mary by the angel Gabriel, the child to be born is designated as "the son of the Highest" by the angelic messenger who does not hesitate to emphasize "that holy thing which shall be born of thee shall be called the Son of God" (1:32, 35).

The Apostle Peter in the course of one of his great sermons in the Book of Acts quotes David in his description of the Messiah as God's "Holy One" (2:27) and reiterates this title in the third chapter as "the Holy One and the Just" (verse 14).

The Apostle John, preaching with Peter further on in the Book of Acts, states in a stirring prayer to God: "For of a truth against thy holy child Jesus, whom thou hast anointed, both Herod, and Pontius Pilate, with the Gentiles, and the people of Israel, were gathered together" (4:27).

The word translated "child" can also be rendered "servant" in Greek, but regardless of which way one takes it, it is qualified by the word "holy" which any lexicon or dictionary defines as "without sin—pure." Our Lord made this claim for Himself when, in conflict with the Jews, He challenged them to dare to accuse Him of sin (John 8:46), and the writer of the epistle to the Hebrews declares Him to be "holy, harmless and undefiled, separate from sinners" (7:26). None of these pronouncements of the Scripture are in agreement with Mr. Armstrong's contention that Jesus Christ had a sinful nature and a character that needed to be perfected due to defects which he implies existed, thereby necessitating a "perfecting" process.

The Worldwide Church of God does indeed honor Christ with its lips, but in the cold analytical dawn of Biblical examination and analysis, there can be little doubt that its heart is far from Him.

There are many other errors in the theology of Mr. Armstrong which could easily fill a small volume, but space does not allow us to deal with it in the confines of a chapter. Let it be said, however, that the theology of Herbert Armstrong and his Worldwide Church of God contains just enough truth to make it attractive to the listener who is unaware of the multiple sources of heretical doctrine he has drawn upon for the balance of his theological system, enough of which permeates both his radio programs and his publications to insure the uninformed listener a gospel of confusion unparalleled in the history of American cultism. The Worldwide Church of God is all the more dangerous as it makes profuse use of the Bible and professes to swear allegiance to only "the plain truth of the Scripture," while, in reality, its allegiance is to the interpretations of the Scripture propagated by Herbert W. Armstrong whom one magazine has aptly described as "Mr. Confusion." Since "God is not the author of confusion," and this "plain truth" no student of the Scripture will deny, there is one sure remedy to the problem of the spread of Mr. Armstrong's religion. Turn off the set and open your Bible, for within its pages God is always broadcasting the eternal message of the Gospel of Grace impregnated by the Spirit of God in every essential necessary to the redemption of the soul and re-creation and living of the Christian life. When this is supplemented by attendance in a truly Christian Church where that Gospel is preached, there is no need to listen to the Herbert Armstrongs of our day, for as the Psalmist so beautifully described it, "the entrance of thy Word giveth light."